epic adventure

Epic Treks

LEWIS & CLARK ▲ LIVINGSTONE & STANLEY
BURKE & WILLS ▲ AMUNDSEN & SCOTT

Published in the United States by Kingfisher,
175 Fifth Ave., New York, NY 10010
Kingfisher is an imprint of Macmillan Children's Books, London.
All rights reserved

Distributed in the U.S. by Macmillan,
175 Fifth Ave., New York, NY 10010
Distributed in Canada by H.B. Fenn and Company Ltd.,
34 Nixon Road, Bolton, Ontario L7E 1W2

Conceived and produced by Weldon Owen Pty Ltd
59-61 Victoria Street, McMahons Point
Sydney, NSW 2060, Australia
Copyright © 2011 Weldon Owen Pty Ltd
First printed 2011

WELDON OWEN PTY LTD
Managing Director Kay Scarlett
Publisher Corinne Roberts
Creative Director Sue Burk

Senior Vice President, International Sales Stuart Laurence
Sales Manager: United States Ellen Towell
Administration Manager, International Sales Kristine Ravn
Production Director Todd Rechner
Production and Prepress Controller Mike Crowton
Production Controller Lisa Conway
Production Coordinator Nathan Grice

Concept Design Arthur Brown/Cooling Brown
Managing Editor Averil Moffat
Project Editor Scott Forbes
Designers Tony Gordon, Mark Thacker
Cartography Will Pringle, Mapgraphx
Art Manager Trucie Henderson
Picture Research Joanna Collard
Editorial Assistant Natalie Ryan

Index Jo Rudd

Library of Congress Cataloging-in-Publication data has been applied for.

ISBN 978-0-7534-6668-1

Kingfisher books are available for special promotions and premiums.
For details contact: Special Markets Department, Macmillan,
175 Fifth Avenue, New York, NY 10010

For more information, please visit www.kingfisherbooks.com

Printed by Toppan Leefung Printing Limited
Manufactured in China

10 9 8 7 6 5 4 3 2 1

A WELDON OWEN PRODUCTION

The paper used in the manufacture of this book is sourced from
wood grown in sustainable forests. It complies with the Environmental
Management System Standard ISO 14001:2004

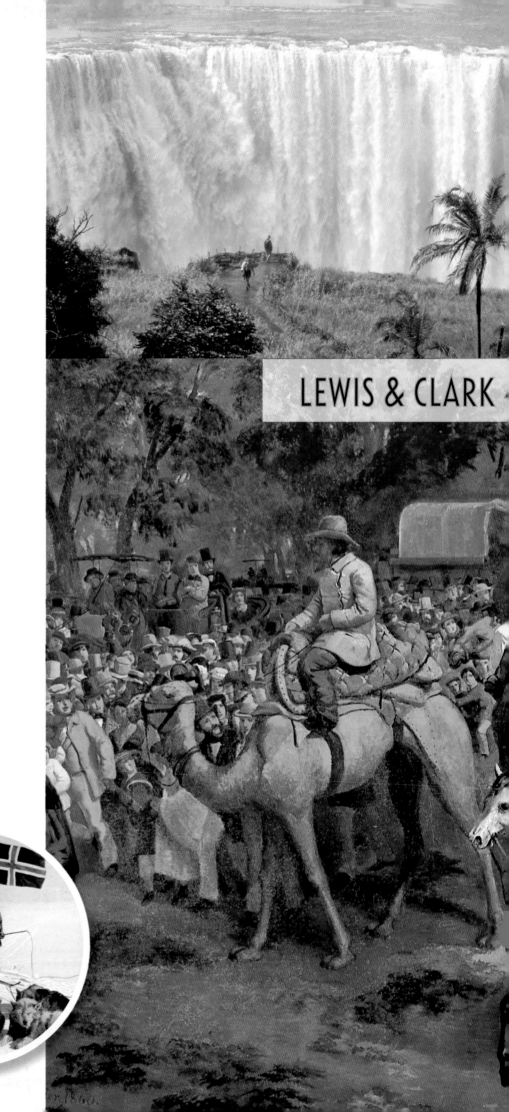

LEWIS & CLARK

Epic Treks

LIVINGSTONE & STANLEY ▲ BURKE & WILLS ▲ AMUNDSEN & SCOTT

Betty Hagglund

KINGFISHER
NEW YORK

introduction

From the earliest times, men and women have explored their world. Some searched for trade routes, lost treasures, or new lands to colonize; others traveled as missionaries, to spread religious beliefs. More than anything else, however, what motivated the greatest explorers was simple curiosity: What was on the other side of that mountain? How wide was North America? Where was the source of the Nile River? In the days before railroads, motor cars, and airplanes, finding out often involved traveling incredible distances overland: on foot, horse, or camel, by wagon or canoe, and for months, even years, at a time. And it usually meant facing severe dangers, extraordinary hardships, and the uncertainty of not knowing when, if ever, you might make it back home.

contents

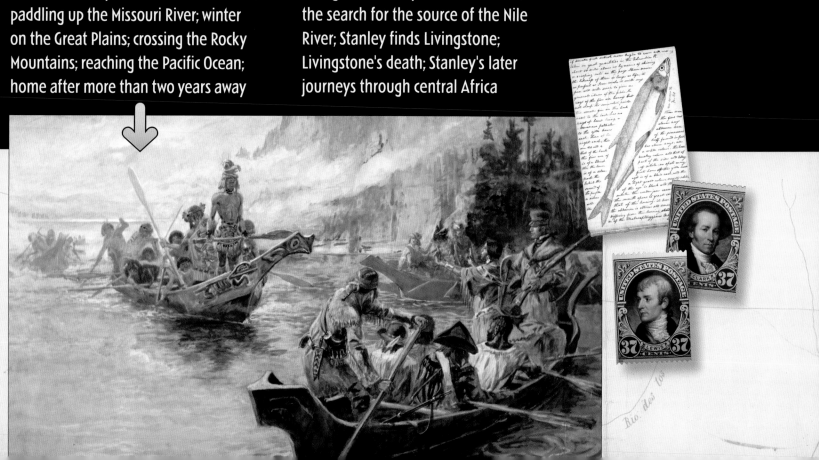

Lewis & Clark
CHARTING THE AMERICAN WEST

The Corps of Discovery

When Thomas Jefferson became president of the United States in 1801, U.S. territory extended only as far west as the Mississippi River. Beyond the Mississippi lay a wilderness, inhabited by hundreds of different American Indian tribes. In 1803, however, Jefferson purchased a huge area of land, known as Louisiana, from France. He then decided to send an exploratory party across this territory. The expedition had four aims: to find a trade route to the Pacific Ocean; to protect American interests against land claims made by Spain, France, and England; to make contact with the scattered American Indian nations; and to map and find out as much as possible about the new territory. Jefferson chose his personal secretary, Meriwether Lewis, to head the expedition, and Lewis asked his friend, William Clark, to join him.

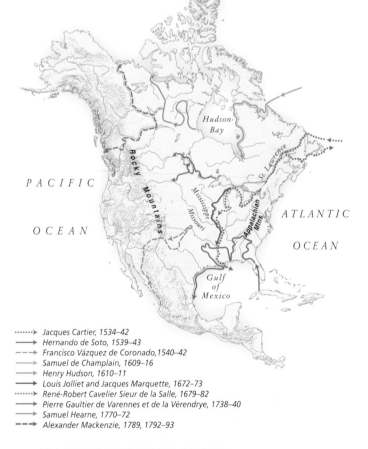

········ Jacques Cartier, 1534–42
⟶ Hernando de Soto, 1539–43
--→ Francisco Vázquez de Coronado,1540–42
--→ Samuel de Champlain, 1609–16
⟶ Henry Hudson, 1610–11
⟶ Louis Jolliet and Jacques Marquette, 1672–73
········ René-Robert Cavelier Sieur de la Salle, 1679–82
⟶ Pierre Gaultier de Varennes et de la Vérendrye, 1738–40
⟶ Samuel Hearne, 1770–72
--→ Alexander Mackenzie, 1789, 1792–93

TRACKS THROUGH THE WILDERNESS
The western interior of North America was largely unexplored by Europeans before Lewis and Clark's expedition, although Spanish, Russian, and British navigators and fur trappers had earlier surveyed the Pacific coast.

The Louisiana Purchase

When Jefferson bought Louisiana from France in 1803 for US$ 15 million, it doubled the size of the United States. There were no roads through this land, and no one was even certain how big it was or what was there. Finding out was part of Lewis and Clark's mission.

British Territory

Oregon Country (claimed by Spain, Britain, USA)

Louisiana Purchase

Spanish Territory

Indiana Territory

VT N.H.
MASS.
N.Y.
R.I.
CONN.
PA
N.J.
OHIO
D.C.
DEL.
VA
MD
KY
N.C.
TENN.
S.C.
GA
Mississippi Territory

West Florida (Spain)

East Florida (Spain)

- ▨ Louisiana Purchase
- ▨ US states
- ▨ US territories
- ☐ Other territories
- ▨ Disputed areas

William Clark

Meriwether Lewis

EXPEDITION FACT FILE

Official members of the Corps	c. 30
Others who joined at various points	c. 20
Duration of expedition	2 years and four months
Distance traveled	10,624 miles (17,098 km)
Deaths	1

A Canine Companion

About 30 men formed the Corps of Discovery, including officers, soldiers, French boatmen, a cook, interpreters, and Clark's African slave, York. They took with them a Newfoundland dog like this one (below), named Seaman, to help with hunting and guarding camps. Seaman survived the whole trip.

CRAFT FOR ALL CONDITIONS

Most of the way would be traveled by river, and the expedition required a variety of boats to cope with the changing conditions. Lewis drew up the designs for the main keelboat (left), but the Corps would also use, at various times, 3 pirogues (large, narrow wooden boats), 16 dugout canoes, at least 5 American Indian canoes, and a number of skin boats and log rafts.

Fully Equipped

The expedition carried over 11 tons (10 t) of supplies, including 50 kegs of pork, 30 barrels of flour, 600 lb (272 kg) of grease, weapons, blankets, medicines, navigational instruments, books, paper, and ink, and gifts for American Indians, such as fishhooks, mirrors, jewelry, and beads. Each man also carried a personal kit of the sort shown at left, including tools, a knife and ax, and flints and tinder for lighting fires.

A pocket compass used on the expedition

The Way West

Lewis planned to follow the Missouri River north and then west, and hoped to find a river route all the way to the Pacific Ocean, via which the United States would then be able to trade with Asia. The Missouri River rises in the Rocky Mountains and plunges down a series of whitewater rapids. It is a powerful river and carries huge quantities of water. The currents were strong and floating logs and branches, unstable banks, and hidden shallows all posed dangers. Even when the men rowed as hard as they could, they managed to travel just a few miles each day.

THE PACIFIC COAST
U.S. ship-captain and navigator Robert Gray had discovered the mouth of the Columbia River in 1792, while exploring the northern Pacific shoreline. British, French, and Russian traders were also active on the coast, but few had ventured inland from there.

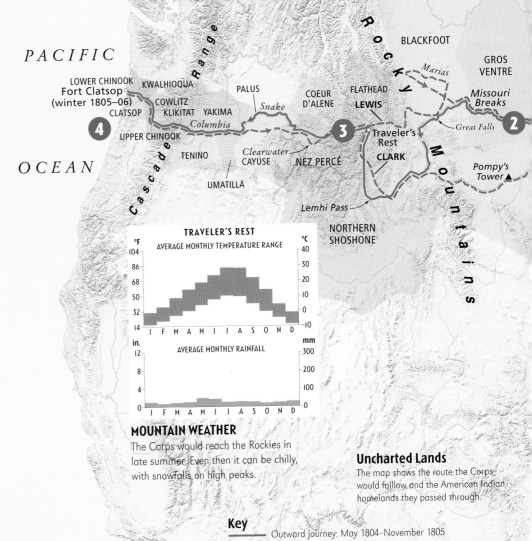

TRAVELER'S REST
AVERAGE MONTHLY TEMPERATURE RANGE

AVERAGE MONTHLY RAINFALL

MOUNTAIN WEATHER
The Corps would reach the Rockies in late summer. Even then it can be chilly, with snowfalls on high peaks.

Uncharted Lands
The map shows the route the Corps would follow and the American Indian homelands they passed through.

Key
— Outward journey: May 1804–November 1805
- - - Return journey: March–September 1806

CROW   Indian homeland

THE ROUTE TODAY
This map shows the route the Corps followed in relation to the present-day U.S. national and state borders.

Native Peoples
During their journey, the explorers would encounter many groups of American Indians and at least eight American Indian languages. The tribes differed from each other in their ways of living and their previous experiences of white people.

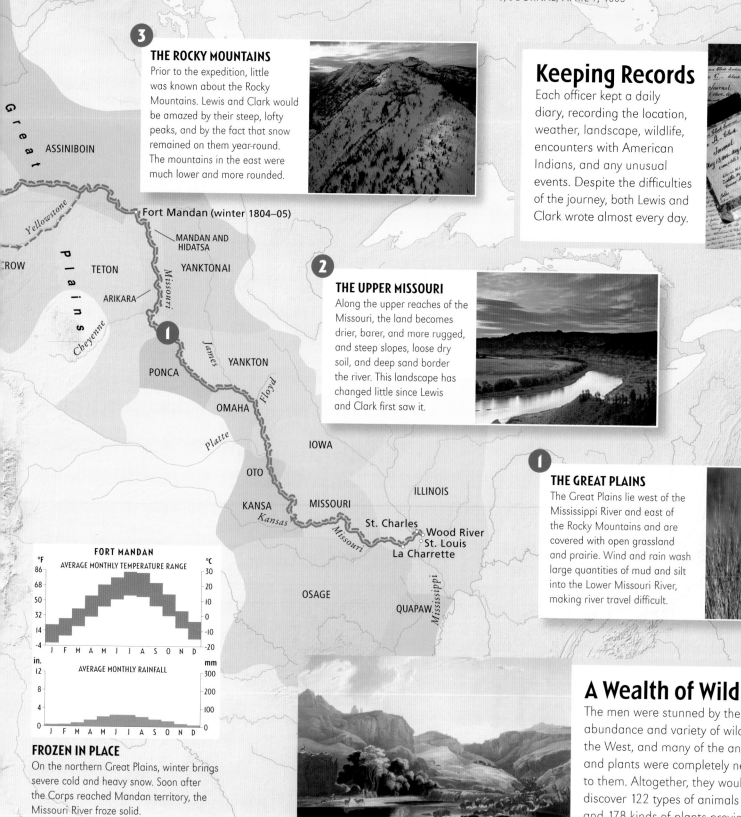

"We were now about to penetrate a country at least 2,000 miles [3,200 km] in width, on which the foot of civilized man had never trod." MERIWETHER LEWIS, JOURNAL, APRIL 7, 1805

3

THE ROCKY MOUNTAINS
Prior to the expedition, little was known about the Rocky Mountains. Lewis and Clark would be amazed by their steep, lofty peaks, and by the fact that snow remained on them year-round. The mountains in the east were much lower and more rounded.

Keeping Records
Each officer kept a daily diary, recording the location, weather, landscape, wildlife, encounters with American Indians, and any unusual events. Despite the difficulties of the journey, both Lewis and Clark wrote almost every day.

Great

ASSINIBOIN

Yellowstone

Fort Mandan (winter 1804–05)

MANDAN AND HIDATSA

P l a i n s

CROW

TETON

YANKTONAI

Missouri

ARIKARA

Cheyenne

1

2

THE UPPER MISSOURI
Along the upper reaches of the Missouri, the land becomes drier, barer, and more rugged, and steep slopes, loose dry soil, and deep sand border the river. This landscape has changed little since Lewis and Clark first saw it.

James

YANKTON

PONCA

Floyd

OMAHA

Platte

IOWA

OTO

ILLINOIS

KANSA

MISSOURI

Kansas

St. Charles

Missouri

Wood River
St. Louis
La Charrette

OSAGE

Mississippi

QUAPAW

1

THE GREAT PLAINS
The Great Plains lie west of the Mississippi River and east of the Rocky Mountains and are covered with open grassland and prairie. Wind and rain wash large quantities of mud and silt into the Lower Missouri River, making river travel difficult.

FORT MANDAN

AVERAGE MONTHLY TEMPERATURE RANGE

°F		°C
86		30
68		20
50		10
32		0
14		-10
-4		-20

J F M A M J J A S O N D

AVERAGE MONTHLY RAINFALL

in.		mm
12		300
8		200
4		100
0		0

J F M A M J J A S O N D

FROZEN IN PLACE
On the northern Great Plains, winter brings severe cold and heavy snow. Soon after the Corps reached Mandan territory, the Missouri River froze solid.

A Wealth of Wildlife
The men were stunned by the abundance and variety of wildlife in the West, and many of the animals and plants were completely new to them. Altogether, they would discover 122 types of animals and 178 kinds of plants previously unknown to Europeans.

Across the Plains

Through the spring, summer, and fall of 1804, the Corps of Discovery traveled up the Missouri River. While most of the men rowed or pulled the boats, others hunted for deer, duck, and geese. Most days, Lewis walked along the shore with Seaman, his dog, making observations of animals and birds, and notes that he later used when drawing maps. In August, one of the men, Sergeant Charles Floyd, fell ill and died. He was buried beside the Missouri River and a nearby stream was named the Floyd River in his honor. The explorers then continued north, through the lands of various Indian peoples, including the Yankton, Arikara, and Teton Sioux. With the weather growing colder, they decided to halt in the territory of the Mandan Indians, and build a fort where they could spend the winter.

Among the Mandan
The Mandans lived in large earth lodges, each housing 20 or more people, and raised crops and hunted buffalo. They were friendly and encouraged the explorers to stay. Their village served as a major marketplace for other American Indians, as well as French and British traders, so they were used to visitors.

A New Threat

As the expedition moved west, it had increasingly frequent and frightening encounters with grizzly bears, which the men had never seen before their trip. Near present-day Culbertson, Montana, on April 29, Lewis was chased 80 yards (73 m) by a bear weighing more than 300 pounds (136 kg), before he managed to shoot it.

THE MISSOURI BREAKS

When the river ice broke up in March, the Corps left Fort Mandan. The keelboat was sent back east; six new canoes and two pirogues were taken west. The expedition passed through treeless plains, thick with buffalo, and beneath gigantic cliffs, today known as the Missouri Breaks, which Lewis described as "beautiful in the extreme."

LIVE SPECIMENS

The Corps sent records and specimens back to President Jefferson, including American Indian artifacts, dried plants, insects, rocks, maps, five live birds, and a live prairie dog like this one.

Native Guide

At Fort Mandan, Lewis and Clark hired a French-Canadian trader, Toussaint Charbonneau, as a guide, mainly because his then-pregnant wife, 15-year-old Sacagawea, was a Shoshone, from the Rocky Mountains, and they knew she would be helpful there. Sacagawea (shown here with Lewis and Clark), who gave birth to a son on February 11, 1805, would prove to be an invaluable guide.

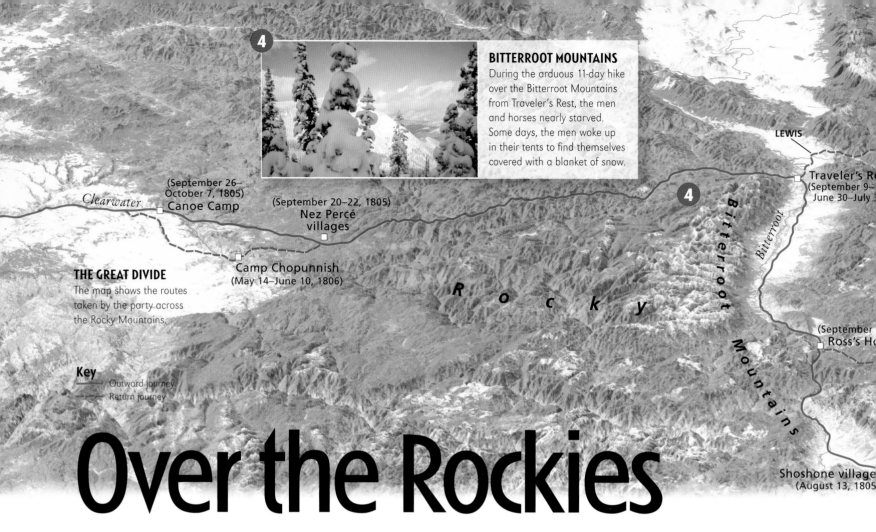

4

BITTERROOT MOUNTAINS
During the arduous 11-day hike over the Bitterroot Mountains from Traveler's Rest, the men and horses nearly starved. Some days, the men woke up in their tents to find themselves covered with a blanket of snow.

LEWIS

Traveler's R
(September 9–
June 30–July

Clearwater

(September 26–
October 7, 1805)
Canoe Camp

(September 20–22, 1805)
Nez Percé
villages

4

Bitterroot

Bitterroot

THE GREAT DIVIDE
The map shows the routes taken by the party across the Rocky Mountains.

Camp Chopunnish
(May 14–June 10, 1806)

R o c k y

(September
Ross's Ho

Key
Outward journey
Return journey

M
o
u
n
t
a
i
n
s

Shoshone village
(August 13, 1805

Over the Rockies

Strong currents and winds made progress slow. The men buried some equipment to use on the way back, which made the boats lighter. But in mid-June they encountered a series of huge waterfalls, today known as Great Falls, and violent storms, which together delayed them by nearly a month. They then entered a range of mountains higher than any they had ever seen: the Rocky Mountains. At a place now called the Three Forks, three rivers met to form the Missouri. They followed the right-hand fork west, but soon realized that they would need horses and local knowledge to get across the mountains. They knew the Shoshone Indians could help, but, frustratingly, could not find them. Finally, on August 13, Lewis located a Shoshone war party and, with Sacagawea's help, obtained horses and guides, who led the Corps over the rest of the ranges.

A CROOKED RIVER
Beyond the Three Forks, the party followed the Jefferson River, which they found to be "very crooked many short bends." There was no sign of the Shoshone. But on August 7, Sacagawea recognized a hill, Beaverhead Rock (at the center of this photograph), which at least meant they were in Shoshone territory.

Missouri

1 Great Falls
(June 13, 1805)

Lewis and
Clark Pass
(July 7, 1806)

Blackfoot

Gates of the
Mountains
(July 19, 1805)

M o u n t a i n s

Missouri

Jefferson

Three Forks (July 27, 1805)

Madison

Gallatin

Beaverhead

Beaverhead Rock
(August 7, 1805)

i Pass
12, 1805)

GREAT FALLS
This series of large waterfalls prevented the Corps ascending the river by boat; instead they had to portage their boats and more than 1 ton (907 kg) of equipment, food, and stores around the falls.

2

Long-lost Brother
The Shoshone Indians were nomadic people, traveling from place to place as they hunted and gathered food. When the expedition found them, they were suspicious. But after Sacagawea recognized their chief, Cameahwait, as her own brother, the Shoshone at once offered to help.

3

LEMHI PASS
From Lemhi Pass, Lewis could see that there were "immence ranges of high mountains still to the West of us," and not just one range as his maps had indicated.

A DIFFERENT STORY
The map carried by the expedition showed the Rockies as a narrow line of mountains, whereas they are 250 miles (400 km) wide where the Corps planned to cross them.

A LONG AND WINDING ROAD
Heading west from Great Falls, the Corps skirted the highest peaks by following the Jefferson River, crossing Lemhi Pass, and then heading north up the Bitterroot Valley. But from Traveler's Rest, they had to climb over the rugged Bitterroot Mountains.

Canoe Camp | Bitterroot Mountains | Bitterroot Valley | Great Falls

10,000 feet (3,000 m)

6,560 feet (2,000 m)

3,280 feet (1,000 m)

0

300 miles (480 km) | 200 miles (320 km) | 100 miles (160 km) | 0

Downriver to the Sea

Emerging from the Bitterroot Mountains, the explorers met Nez Percé Indians, who gave them food, drew them maps, and helped them make new canoes. The Corps then followed the fast-flowing Clearwater, Snake, and Columbia rivers, portaging when the way was too rocky, lowering their boats down high waterfalls with ropes, and stopping frequently to trade with American Indians. The scenery changed, from barren highlands to lush forests. One day, they realized that the Columbia was rising and falling with the ocean's tides and that they could hear the sound of waves. Storms and drifting logs pinned them in the river for another five days, but on November 18, Lewis, scouting ahead, saw the Pacific Ocean for the first time and carved his name on a tree in celebration.

CULTURES OF THE COLUMBIA
Many tribes along the Columbia, such as the Yakima and Chinook, were friendly, and Lewis and Clark took a strong interest in their cultures. Clark made sketches of the Chinook practice of head flattening, whereby a board was placed across a baby's head and gradually tightened to flatten the front of the head. The Chinook considered this handsome and a mark of high status.

THE COLUMBIA RIVER GORGE
In the Cascade Range, the Columbia has carved a deep gorge with walls that rise up to 4,000 feet (1,200 m) above the river.

"Ocian in view! O! the joy." WILLIAM CLARK, JOURNAL

The River's Bounty

Lewis and Clark were amazed by the huge numbers of fish, especially salmon and trout, that the American Indians caught in the Columbia. Lewis made this sketch of a fatty fish called a euchalon. It could be eaten—Lewis said it was "superior to any fish I ever tasted"—but also dried and, by attaching a wick to it, used as a candle. Many of the American Indians who live along the river today still fish as their ancestors did (far right).

Winter at Fort Clatsop

The Corps built a fort on the south side of the Columbia River as their home for the winter. They moved in on Christmas Eve, and for the next three months spent their days hunting, fishing, and repairing their canoes and other equipment. By candlelight, Lewis wrote detailed descriptions of the animals, plants, and people he had seen, while Clark drew maps of the area (below).

EXPLORING THE COAST

The men eagerly explored the Pacific shore and, as Clark wrote, appeared "much satisfied with their trip, beholding with astonishment the high waves dashing against the rocks." But it rained almost every day during the four and a half months the Corps spent on the coast, making some of the men ill and all of them wet and miserable.

Back from the Dead

By the time the men left Fort Clatsop in late March 1806, many people back home had given them up for dead. Glad to get away from the constant rain on the coast, they traveled slowly back up the Columbia. It was too early in the year for salmon fishing and game was scarce; many American Indians they met were dying of hunger. In May, they tried to cross the Bitterroot Mountains, but huge snowdrifts made them turn back; a few weeks later, three American Indian guides got them through. Lewis and Clark then decided to follow separate routes: Lewis went north to explore the Marias River and Clark followed the Yellowstone. They reunited on August 12 and traveled downstream to St. Louis, to be welcomed by cheering crowds on September 23. They had been gone for nearly two and a half years.

FIRST BLOOD
On July 26, 1806, near the Marias River, Lewis and his men met eight Blackfoot Indians. The Blackfoot were enemies to the Shoshone and the Nez Percé, friends of the Corps. At dawn next day, some of the Blackfoot tried to steal the explorers' horses and guns. One of Lewis's men stabbed a Blackfoot in the heart and Lewis shot another in the stomach. It was the only fight with American Indians during the whole trip.

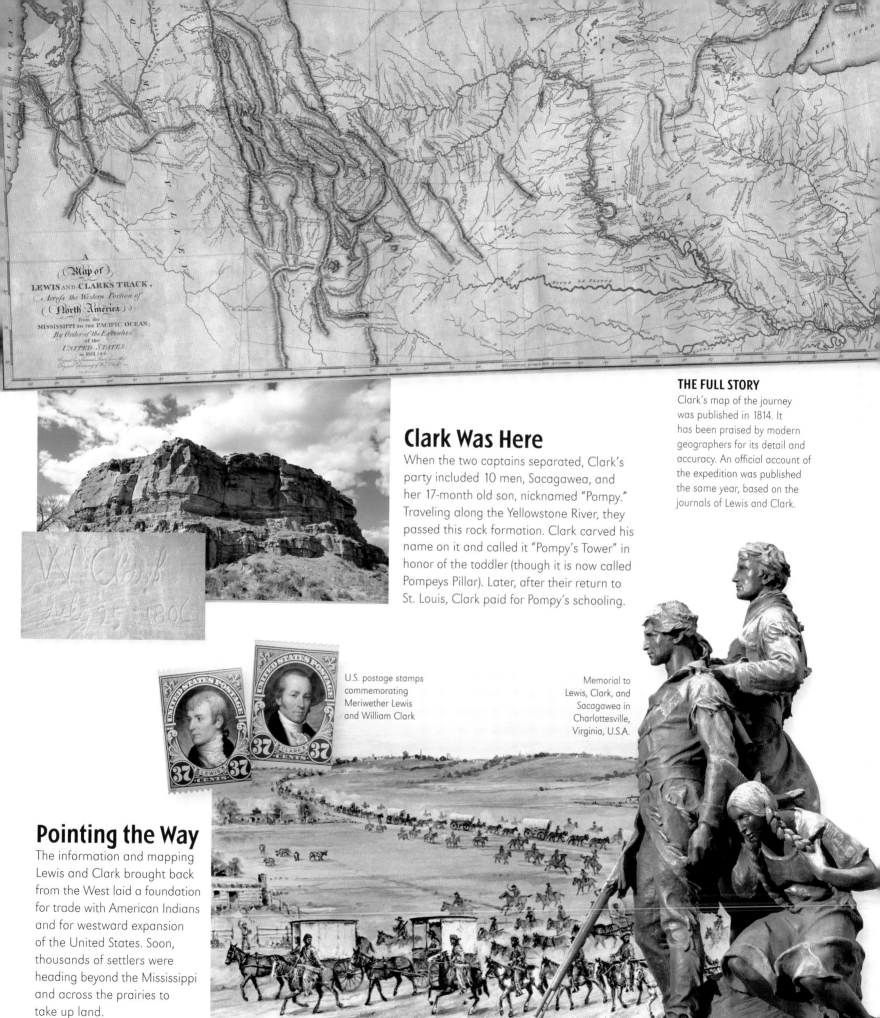

Clark Was Here

When the two captains separated, Clark's party included 10 men, Sacagawea, and her 17-month old son, nicknamed "Pompy." Traveling along the Yellowstone River, they passed this rock formation. Clark carved his name on it and called it "Pompy's Tower" in honor of the toddler (though it is now called Pompeys Pillar). Later, after their return to St. Louis, Clark paid for Pompy's schooling.

THE FULL STORY
Clark's map of the journey was published in 1814. It has been praised by modern geographers for its detail and accuracy. An official account of the expedition was published the same year, based on the journals of Lewis and Clark.

U.S. postage stamps commemorating Meriwether Lewis and William Clark

Memorial to Lewis, Clark, and Sacagawea in Charlottesville, Virginia, U.S.A.

Pointing the Way

The information and mapping Lewis and Clark brought back from the West laid a foundation for trade with American Indians and for westward expansion of the United States. Soon, thousands of settlers were heading beyond the Mississippi and across the prairies to take up land.

Livingstone & Stanley

INTO THE HEART OF AFRICA

Fraught with Peril

By the early 19th century, Europeans had mapped, explored, and begun to colonize the coastline of Africa, but the interior remained mainly unexplored, unmapped—and perilous. Two men did more than others to change this: David Livingstone and Henry Morton Stanley. Livingstone traveled to Africa as a missionary and became the first European to cross the central interior from coast to coast. He befriended African chiefs, and campaigned against the slave trade. After he disappeared in 1867, Stanley traveled to Africa to search for him, and later went on to explore vast areas of central Africa himself. The meeting of Livingstone and Stanley, near Lake Tanganyika in 1871, would become one of the most famous encounters in the history of exploration.

THE LION'S DEN
In 1844, David Livingstone was attacked by a lion, but was saved by his African friend, Mebalwe, and a group of tribesmen. Livingstone recovered, but his arm gave him pain for the rest of his life.

David Livingstone

Henry Morton Stanley

Missionary and Reporter
As a poor Scottish boy, Livingstone had to work by day and attend school at night. He trained as a doctor and missionary, and went to work in Africa in 1841. Stanley, an illegitimate child, was educated in a workhouse. He left Britain for America in 1858, fought in the American Civil War, and then became a reporter.

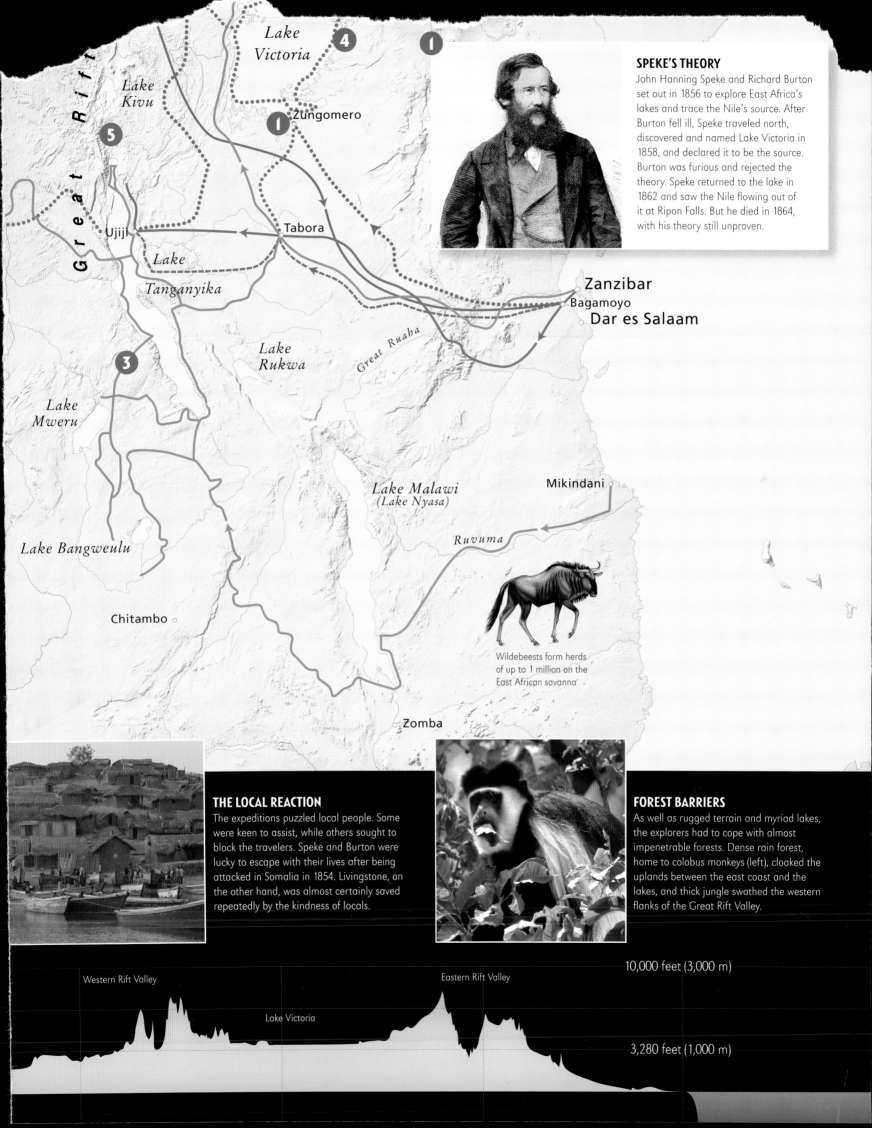

Lake Victoria

Lake Kivu

Great Rift

④

①

⑤

Zungomero

①

Ujiji

Lake Tanganyika

Tabora

③

Lake Rukwa

Great Ruaha

Zanzibar
Bagamoyo
Dar es Salaam

Lake Mweru

Lake Malawi
(Lake Nyasa)

Mikindani

Ruvuma

Lake Bangweulu

Chitambo

Zomba

SPEKE'S THEORY

John Hanning Speke and Richard Burton set out in 1856 to explore East Africa's lakes and trace the Nile's source. After Burton fell ill, Speke traveled north, discovered and named Lake Victoria in 1858, and declared it to be the source. Burton was furious and rejected the theory. Speke returned to the lake in 1862 and saw the Nile flowing out of it at Ripon Falls. But he died in 1864, with his theory still unproven.

Wildebeests form herds of up to 1 million on the East African savanna

THE LOCAL REACTION

The expeditions puzzled local people. Some were keen to assist, while others sought to block the travelers. Speke and Burton were lucky to escape with their lives after being attacked in Somalia in 1854. Livingstone, on the other hand, was almost certainly saved repeatedly by the kindness of locals.

FOREST BARRIERS

As well as rugged terrain and myriad lakes, the explorers had to cope with almost impenetrable forests. Dense rain forest, home to colobus monkeys (left), cloaked the uplands between the east coast and the lakes, and thick jungle swathed the western flanks of the Great Rift Valley.

10,000 feet (3,000 m)

Western Rift Valley

Eastern Rift Valley

Lake Victoria

3,280 feet (1,000 m)

A Dangerous Place

Most early European exploration of Africa took place in the north of the continent, and, even by the mid-19th century, little of the interior had been explored. Central Africa in particular was full of perils—dangerous animals, swamps and dense forests, and deadly diseases such as malaria.

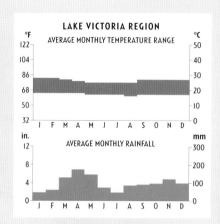

LAKE VICTORIA REGION
AVERAGE MONTHLY TEMPERATURE RANGE

AVERAGE MONTHLY RAINFALL

HOT AND HUMID
The climate of central Africa is generally hot and wet. European explorers found it exhausting.

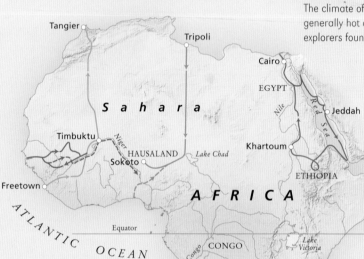

- James Bruce, 1768–73
- Mungo Park, 1795–96
- Mungo Park, 1805–06
- Hugh Clapperton, Walter Oudney, and Dixon Denham, 1822–25
- Hugh Clapperton and Richard Lander, 1825–27
- René Caillié, 1827–28

THE NILE MYSTERY
The continent's and the world's longest river, the Nile flows from the central African interior north to Egypt. The location of its starting point was a mystery that intrigued Greek and Roman geographers, and inspired early European expeditions to Africa, including that of Scotsman James Bruce in 1768–73.

HARD GOING
During his travels in northwestern Africa, Scottish explorer Mungo Park (1771–1806) often became seriously ill. Nevertheless, he compiled detailed descriptions of the region. He drowned on his second expedition, when his canoe was ambushed.

On Their Guard
The transatlantic slave trade and European settlement had brought great upheaval and conflict to Africa. As a result, the peoples of the African interior were on their guard when strangers arrived, and quick to defend themselves.

A traditional African mask from Zaire

ile River

The White Nile

The White Nile, seen here in Uganda, is the longer of the Nile River's two major tributaries, the shorter one being the Blue Nile. The source of the Blue Nile in Ethiopia, described by 17th-century missionaries, was rediscovered by James Bruce in 1770, but the source of the White Nile remained a mystery.

The Great Rift Valley

Central Africa's most striking geographical feature is the Great Rift Valley, a system of cracks in Earth's surface that runs for nearly 4,000 miles (6,400 km) down the eastern side of the continent. In East Africa, the Rift Valley splits into two branches flanked by mountains. Many of these mountains are so high that although they are near the equator, they have snow on their peaks year-round.

Obb

White Nile

2

V a l l e y

2 *Murchison Falls*

L. Kyoga

L. Albert

Mt Stanley ▲ Kampala

Ripon Falls

Lake Edward

Usumbura

FOLLOWING THE RIVER

Samuel and Florence Baker followed the Nile upstream from Cairo for three years (1861–64). They overcame many obstacles, including illness, difficult terrain, and obstructive local chiefs, to reach Lake Albert, and nearby Murchison Falls, a dramatic waterfall in a narrow gorge. But they were still some 300 miles (500 km) from the river's outlet from Lake Victoria, and could go no farther.

THE ZAMBEZI EXPEDITION

The aim of the 1858 Zambezi Expedition was to find river routes for British trade, so Livingstone took a steam launch, the *Ma Robert*. However, he found the Zambezi, Shire, and Ruvuma rivers to be unnavigable due to the presence of rapids. Mary came to join her husband in 1861, and he was devastated when she died of a fever the following year. In 1864, the government recalled the expedition and Livingstone made his way back to Britain.

A boat's compass used on the first journey made by Livingstone (top) and a sextant used by Livingstone in central Africa (above)

Determined and Respectful

Livingstone's early success was due partly to the respect with which he treated African people. He studied their languages and cultures, and employed many of them alongside a small number of Europeans. He carried few arms and was careful not to overreact to aggression. He was also a skilled navigator, as well as being resilient and very determined.

EARLY TRAVELS

Livingstone's first major expedition, to Lake Ngami in 1849 (below), fired his determination to find a river route across central Africa. The search took him to the Zambezi River, to the west coast at Luanda, and back across the continent to the eastern port of Quelimane.

The Slave Trade

Traveling deeper into Africa than most other Europeans, Livingstone saw and reported the results of the slave trade: captives being marched in chains, villages emptied of people, dead bodies lying unburied. He believed that the best way to undermine the slave trade was to develop other, more legitimate forms of commerce with Africa.

> *"I have satisfactory evidence that Dr. Livingstone was not murdered but had gone on in safety far beyond."*

REPORT OF THE LIVINGSTONE SEARCH EXPEDITION, 1868

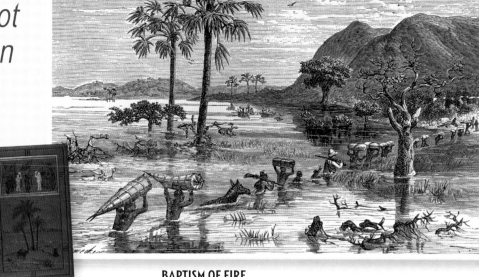

The Full Story
Stanley's book, *How I Found Livingstone*, published in 1872, was a huge success, bringing him both fame and wealth.

BAPTISM OF FIRE
Stanley's first major expedition was extremely challenging and he had to show strong leadership to reach his goals.

The Meeting at Ujiji

When Stanley arrived at Ujiji, Livingstone's men came running to tell him that someone was coming. Stanley pushed his way through the crowds of villagers toward the elderly white man. One of his porters carried a large US flag. Stanley could see that the other man was pale and tired, and that his hat and clothes were old and faded. Stanley walked up to the man, took off his own hat, and said, "Dr. Livingstone, I presume?" When Livingstone said "Yes," they grasped each other's hands and smiled.

HATS OFF
When the two men met, Livingstone was wearing this blue cap and Stanley was wearing a pith helmet like the one shown here.

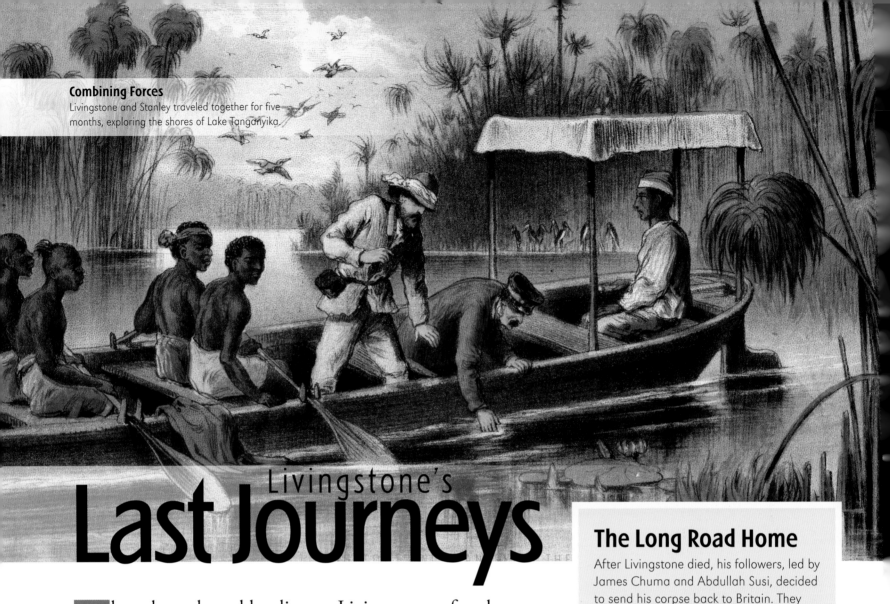

Livingstone's Last Journeys

Though weakened by disease, Livingstone refused to go back to Britain with Stanley; instead, the two men went exploring together. After they parted in March 1872, Livingstone tried to find the source of the Lualaba River. The terrain was difficult, there were heavy rains, the maps were inaccurate, and he became even sicker. On April 30, 1873, he died at a village near Lake Bangweulu. His heart was buried in Africa, but his body was returned to Britain and interred in Westminster Abbey in London. Livingstone's example inspired other explorers and missionaries, many of whom would help bring education and medicine to Africa. His reports of the horrors of slavery led to the end of slave trading on the east coast, while his belief that European trade would be beneficial for the continent led to the establishment of British colonies in central Africa.

The Long Road Home

After Livingstone died, his followers, led by James Chuma and Abdullah Susi, decided to send his corpse back to Britain. They preserved the body, using salt and brandy, and wrapped it in cloth. Then they carried it 1,000 miles (1,600 km) to the east coast. The journey took nine months, and 10 men died. At Bagamoyo, the body was placed in a coffin on a ship bound for England.

Loyal Servants

Following Livingstone's funeral, one of his friends brought Chuma and Susi to England. There, they met Livingstone's family and helped edit his papers. After returning to Africa, Susi joined Stanley's 1874 Trans-Africa Expedition and Chuma worked for European explorers as a caravan leader.

HONORING HIS FOLLOWERS

The Royal Geographical Society presented this special medal to each of the 60 men who had helped carry Livingstone's body across Africa.

"This is the sort of grave I should prefer: to lie in the still, still forest and no hand ever disturb my bones." DAVID LIVINGSTONE, JOURNAL, 1868

HEART OF AFRICA

Livingstone's heart was buried beneath a Mupundu tree at the spot where he died. One of his men carved an inscription, "Livingstone May 4, 1873," and added the names of three of his followers. When the tree decayed, it was chopped down and the inscription was sent to the Royal Geographical Society in London.

A Lasting Legacy

Biographies of Livingstone remained popular long after his death and his influence also endured. Two months after he died, the great slave market at Zanzibar was closed forever.

In Memoriam

Many places in Africa are named for Livingstone and there are memorials to him all over the world, including this statue next to Victoria Falls.

Coast to Coast

Sponsored by two newspapers to resolve questions of African geography, Stanley returned to Africa in 1874. Starting from Zanzibar, he reached Lake Victoria and Ripon Falls, confirming that the White Nile leaves the lake there. Then he made an incredible and dangerous journey along the Lualaba and Congo rivers to the west coast. His last African expedition, which took place between 1886 and 1890, crossed the continent to rescue Emin Pasha, the governor of Equatoria (then an Egyptian province and now part of northern Uganda and southern Sudan) from an uprising. This trip gave rise to Stanley's bestselling book, *In Darkest Africa*.

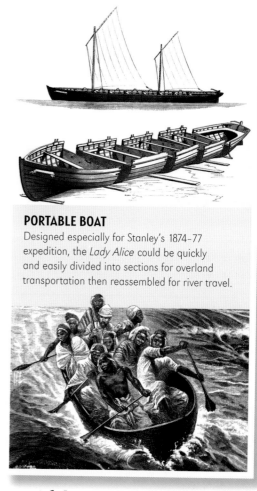

PORTABLE BOAT
Designed especially for Stanley's 1874-77 expedition, the *Lady Alice* could be quickly and easily divided into sections for overland transportation then reassembled for river travel.

The Trans-Africa Expedition

Stanley's 1874-77 expedition across Africa took him and his party through dangerous, uncharted territory. Of the 225 or so men who set out with Stanley, at least 108 died en route.

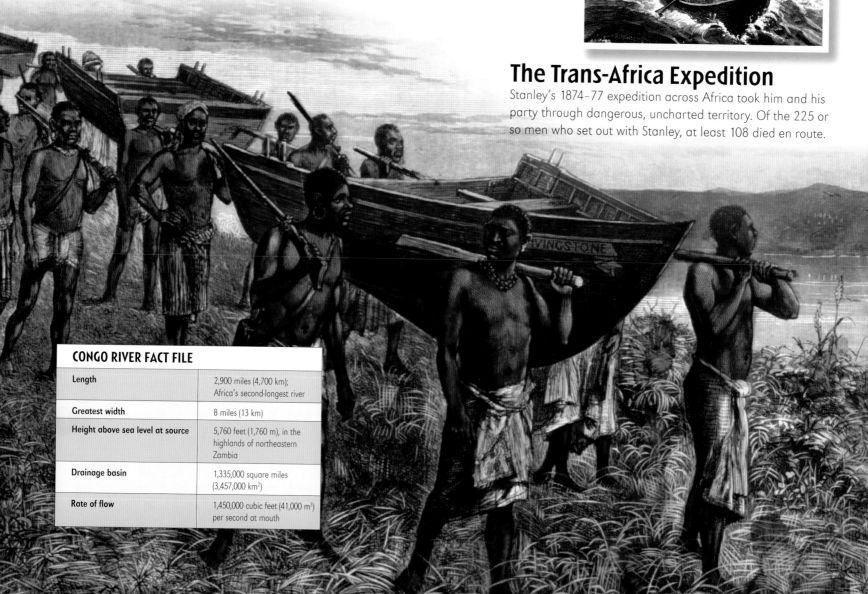

CONGO RIVER FACT FILE	
Length	2,900 miles (4,700 km); Africa's second-longest river
Greatest width	8 miles (13 km)
Height above sea level at source	5,760 feet (1,760 m), in the highlands of northeastern Zambia
Drainage basin	1,335,000 square miles (3,457,000 km²)
Rate of flow	1,450,000 cubic feet (41,000 m³) per second at mouth

The Emin Pasha Relief Expedition

In 1886, traveling to assist Emin Pasha, Stanley approached Equatoria via the river Congo and the Ituri Forest—an indirect, dangerous, and difficult route. The huge, heavily armed expedition was beset by disease, hunger, and warfare, and two-thirds of the men died. Nevertheless, Stanley not only rescued Emin Pasha, but also made a host of significant geographical discoveries along the way.

The cover of Stanley's *In Darkest Africa*

Boots worn by Stanley during his African travels

BATTLING THROUGH
Stanley's party spent five months hacking its way through the dense Ituri Forest and repelling attacks from forest tribes.

The Mountains of the Moon

The ancient Greeks believed that the Nile had its source in rivers flowing from snow-capped mountains called the Mountains of the Moon. The Ruwenzori Range, west of Lake Victoria, which was skirted by Stanley during the Emin Pasha Expedition, was almost certainly the origin of this story. Its highest peak, Mount Stanley, is now named after the explorer.

FAME AND NOTORIETY
Huge crowds came to hear Stanley speak about his expeditions and he received numerous honors and awards. However, some of those who had traveled with him complained that he had used unnecessary violence and that he was a poor leader. His reputation was undermined by these attacks, and when he died in 1904 a request to have his body buried in Westminster Abbey was refused.

Burke & Wills

CROSSING AUSTRALIA

The Victorian
Exploring Expedition

Europeans first visited Australia in 1606. After the first settlers arrived in 1788, explorers began to travel inland, but 70 years later still no one had crossed the interior. The center of the continent remained a mystery, often described as "the ghastly blank." In 1860, the leaders of the newly formed colony of Victoria decided to change that. Gold mines had brought Victoria wealth, and the colonists hoped that a successful exploration of the interior might yield more gold, as well as grazing land, and map a route for a transcontinental telegraph line that would connect Victoria to Britain. Local scientists and businessmen raised money for an expedition to the north coast, dubbed the Victorian Exploring Expedition, and appointed Robert O'Hara Burke to lead it. When the expedition departed, on August 20, 1860, 15,000 people turned out to see it off.

THE START FROM THE PARK
A colorful, boisterous crowd watched and a band played as Burke led the expedition out of Royal Park in central Melbourne.

EXPEDITION FACT FILE	
No. of expeditioners at start	19
Duration of expedition	16 months
Distance traveled	c. 1,865 miles (3,000 km)
Deaths	7
No. who completed expedition	1

Inquisitive to the End

At their camp at Bulloo Lakes, Wright and his men were beset by disease and plagues of rats. Among the sick was Ludwig Becker, who nevertheless continued to write and paint images like this, even when he could barely sit up. He died on April 29, 1861.

Lost Leader

Wills became so feeble that Burke and King went to seek help from the local Aborigines. When Burke grew too weak to stand, he asked King to leave him alone with his pistol. Part of his last letter (right) read, "King has behaved nobly and ... has stayed with me till the last."

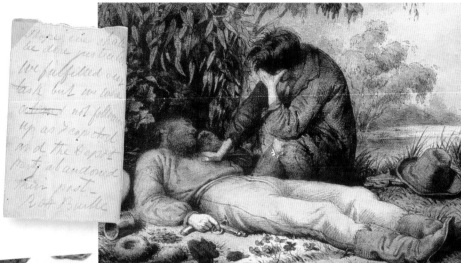

The Death of Wills

King went back to Wills and found that he too had died, and his body had been covered with branches by Aborigines. King was now alone. He took a letter Wills had left for his father, which began, "These are probably the last lines you will ever get from me. We are on the point of starvation." It ended, "Spirits are excellent."

BEARER OF BAD NEWS

By the time Burke and Wills died, Brahe's and Wright's parties had struggled back to Menindee. Brahe then rode on to Melbourne bearing news of the expedition's failure.

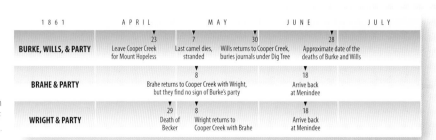

1861	APRIL	MAY	JUNE	JULY
BURKE, WILLS, & PARTY	23 — Leave Cooper Creek for Mount Hopeless	7 — Last camel dies, stranded / 30 — Wills returns to Cooper Creek, buries journals under Dig Tree	28 — Approximate date of the deaths of Burke and Wills	
BRAHE & PARTY		8 — Brahe returns to Cooper Creek with Wright, but they find no sign of Burke's party	18 — Arrive back at Menindee	
WRIGHT & PARTY	29 — Death of Becker	8 — Wright returns to Cooper Creek with Brahe	18 — Arrive back at Menindee	

Rescue and
Remembrance

By June 1861, there had been no news in Melbourne from any of the explorers for six months, and public concern began to mount. Belatedly, the Victorian Exploration Committee and the governments of South Australia and Queensland sent out rescue expeditions. The Victorian party, led by Alfred Howitt, found King and sent news that Burke and Wills were dead. Howitt later brought their bodies home for a huge state funeral in Melbourne, and the two men were mourned as tragic heroes. Nevertheless, there was an investigation of what had gone wrong, and Burke, Brahe, and Wright were all criticized for their actions. The expedition had, however, filled out the map of the Australian interior, proving that there was no inland sea; and the rescue expeditions expanded that knowledge even further.

THE RESCUE PARTIES
Alfred Howitt's expedition reached the Dig Tree in September 1861 and found John King. Meanwhile, other relief expeditions traveled to the Gulf—one overland from the east coast and another by sea—and search parties set out from Queensland and South Australia. These expeditions contributed greatly to knowledge of the interior.

Compass carried by Howitt's party

Sole Survivor

King had survived with the help of the Aborigines, but he was so ill when rescued that Howitt thought he might not survive. Although he grew stronger after a few days, he was mentally and physically damaged by his ordeal, and was not keen to talk about his exploits when he returned to Melbourne, despite being greeted as a hero. He never fully recovered his health, and died aged 33.

STUART'S SUCCESS

John McDouall Stuart and his party had begun their attempt at the south-north crossing on January 1, 1861, but, due to heat, lack of water, and hostile Aborigines returned to Adelaide. They set off again in October, made it to the north coast in July 1862, and returned to Adelaide in triumph—on the day of Burke and Wills's funeral.

This brass plate bearing the initials of Burke and Wills was attached to the box containing their remains.

State Funeral

A public burial and a memorial were planned for Burke and Wills. Howitt brought the men's bones back to Melbourne and on January 21, 1863, Victoria held its first state funeral. Sixty thousand people watched the procession, which was headed by a huge funeral car.

THE LEGEND LIVES ON

A grand memorial statue was erected in Melbourne, showing Burke looking into the distance, and Wills writing in his field book.

Amundsen & Scott

RACE TO THE SOUTH POLE

The Unknown Southern Land

A WORLD OF ICE
Almost all (98 percent) of Antarctica is covered by ice, much of it more than 1½ miles (2.5 km) thick. In the winter, the sea freezes, forming pack ice—huge pieces of floating ice that cover the water.

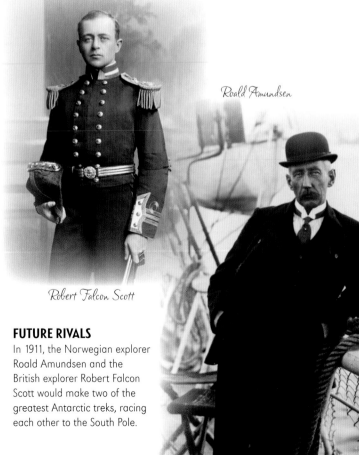

Roald Amundsen

Robert Falcon Scott

ntarctica is the coldest continent on Earth, and wind, snow, ice, and cloud make its climate one of the most treacherous in the world. It was the last continent to be discovered and the last to be explored. Even now, no one lives there permanently, although many scientists spend time working there. Early geographers believed that evidence pointed to the existence of an "unknown southern land," but no one went near enough to see it until the late 18th century. Sailors continued to visit the seas around Antarctica through the 19th century, some exploring, others hunting seals. At the end of that century, the first land-based explorations were made and what became known as the "Heroic Age" of Antarctic exploration began, with countries and explorers competing to make new discoveries.

FUTURE RIVALS
In 1911, the Norwegian explorer Roald Amundsen and the British explorer Robert Falcon Scott would make two of the greatest Antarctic treks, racing each other to the South Pole.

48

DICING WITH DANGER

French explorer Jules Dumont d'Urville's fleet skirted the coast of Antarctica in 1838–40. Wooden ships like these could easily be crushed by pack ice.

AMUNDSEN'S FIRST VISIT

In 1897, Belgian Adrien de Gerlache led an expedition to Antarctica aboard the *Belgica*. Roald Amundsen was one of the crew. In March 1898, the ship was trapped by pack ice. The men developed scurvy, and found the isolation and darkness almost unbearable. It was more than a year before they escaped.

First Sightings

In 1772–75, James Cook sailed the seas around Antarctica, but saw no land. In 1819, Russian explorer Thaddeus von Bellingshausen spent two years sailing round the continent, and in the next 25 years France, Britain, and the United States all sent out expeditions. Even by 1900, however, only a tiny bit of the land had been explored.

→ Thaddeus von Bellingshausen, 1819–21
→ James Weddell, 1823
→ Jules Dumont d'Urville, 1838–40
→ Charles Wilkes, 1839–40
→ James Clark Ross, 1840–43
→ Adrien de Gerlache, 1898–99
→ Carsten Borchgrevink, 1900

North America   **Europe**   **Australia**   **Antarctica**

A Vast, Empty Land

Virtually uninhabited, Antarctica is the fifth-largest continent: smaller than Asia, Africa, North America, and South America, but larger than Europe and Australia.

Scott Blazes a Trail

The first major land exploration was carried out by the British National Antarctic Expedition of 1901–04, led by Robert Scott. At the Bay of Whales, Scott went up in a tethered hydrogen balloon so that he could look into the interior. From Ross Island, the expedition made two trips by dog sled, going farther inland than anyone had done before.

Eyes on the Prize

By the beginning of the 20th century, the main goal for Antarctic explorers was reaching the South Pole. Ernest Shackleton had been with Scott in 1902, but the two men had quarreled and Shackleton had decided he would get to the pole first. By 1907, he had managed to raise money to equip an old sailing ship, the *Nimrod*, and return to Antarctica. Although he got farther than Scott had, he decided to turn back about 100 miles (160 km) from the pole rather than risk the lives of his men. Determined to beat his rival, Scott organized another expedition, sailing on the *Terra Nova*, and reached Antarctica in January 1911. Just as he arrived, Amundsen decided that he too would try to reach the pole.

THE NIMROD EXPEDITION
Shackleton and his men took with them a prefabricated hut (left), which they erected at Cape Royds on Ross Island. Measuring just 33 by 19 feet (10 by 5.8 m), it was cramped for 21 men and their equipment. The hut still stands and is visited regularly by tourists.

Pointing the Way
Shackleton's team reached their farthest point south on January 9, 1909. They hoisted a British flag and took this photograph before turning back.

Heavy Weather

To prepare for his assault on the South Pole, Scott gave himself only nine months—most polar explorers took two years—and he spent little time on research and training. The equipment he took along was heavy, which in turn slowed the *Terra Nova*. After leaving New Zealand, the ship hit a dreadful storm and then became trapped in pack ice for three weeks. At last, on January 4, 1911, Scott and his men landed at Cape Evans on Ross Island.

NATIONAL PRIDE

Several other national expeditions were taking place at the time, including the Scottish National Antarctic Expedition of 1902–04. Its official piper was photographed playing the bagpipes while wearing full Highland dress.

PATH TO THE POLE

As well as blazing a trail toward the pole, Shackleton's expedition climbed Mount Erebus and reached the South Magnetic Pole.

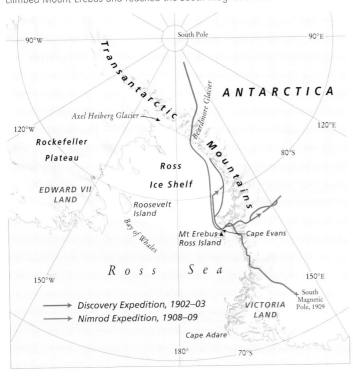

The Race is On

In 1910, Amundsen set off in his ship, the *Fram*, saying he was going to explore the North Pole. But once at sea, he changed course and headed south. Soon after, he sent a message to Scott to say that he was on his way. Scott knew what that meant: Amundsen was trying to beat him to the pole. The race had begun!

Vital Research

Earlier, Amundsen and his men had spent six months with the Inuits in northern Canada, learning Arctic survival skills, an experience that would prove invaluable.

> *"The Antarctic is the most beautiful thing in the world."* APSLEY CHERRY-GARRARD

ANTARCTIC WINTER
At the edge of the Ross Ice Shelf in winter (March to September), long hours of darkness are broken only by spells of twilight.

The Long Wait

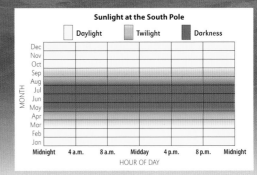

Three-month Night
At the South Pole, it is dark 24 hours a day from mid-May to early August. During the Antarctic summer (October to February), the sun never sets.

Amundsen and his men reached Antarctica on January 14, 1911, and set up their base at the Bay of Whales. Both the British and Norwegian expeditions then rushed to stock depot camps along their chosen routes to the pole before the start of winter, in March. Amundsen's party approached the task in a highly organized way, placing markers to help them find the depots later. The Norwegians were good skiers and completed the job quickly. In contrast, Scott's men struggled. The sea ice had melted, making it difficult to get from Ross Island to the mainland, and their ponies sank in the snow. They placed few markers and built their main depot farther away from the pole than they had originally planned.

Setting up Home
Amundsen's base camp, Framheim, was located on pack ice at the Bay of Whales. There was a risk that the ice might break away and float out to sea, but this site was 60 miles (100 km) closer to the South Pole than Ross Island.

52

Winter Routines

Scott's party built its base at Cape Evans, where it still stands. During the winter, both expeditions worked on repairing and adapting equipment and making everything ready for the trip south. Both parties had plenty of food, but Amundsen wisely had his men eat fresh seal meat every day, which provided abundant vitamin C.

Animal Matters

Amundsen had learned from the Inuit how to drive dog sleds, and he took 97 Greenland husky dogs (left) to haul his sleds. Scott brought some dogs but also ponies (right), which he believed could carry heavier loads. However, the dogs could eat seals and penguins, whereas food for the ponies had to be brought from England.

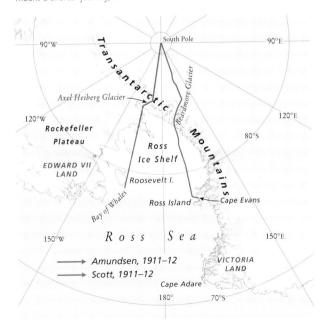

Scott's boots (above) and a medicine chest carried by the expedition (left)

Two Ways to the Pole

Scott planned to follow Shackleton's route toward the pole, via the Beardmore Glacier. Amundsen's route over the Axel Heiberg Glacier meant a shorter journey, but was untried and therefore riskier.

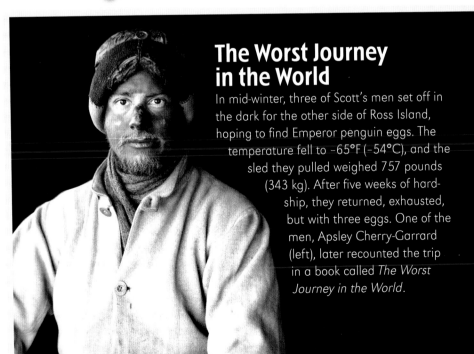

90°W · 90°E
South Pole
Transantarctic
Axel Heiberg Glacier
Beardmore Glacier
120°W · 120°E
Rockefeller
Plateau
80°S
Ross
Ice Shelf
Mountains
EDWARD VII
LAND
Roosevelt I.
Bay of Whales
Ross Island · Cape Evans
150°W
Ross Sea
150°E
→ Amundsen, 1911–12
→ Scott, 1911–12
VICTORIA
LAND
Cape Adare
180° · 70°S

The Worst Journey in the World

In mid-winter, three of Scott's men set off in the dark for the other side of Ross Island, hoping to find Emperor penguin eggs. The temperature fell to -65°F (-54°C), and the sled they pulled weighed 757 pounds (343 kg). After five weeks of hardship, they returned, exhausted, but with three eggs. One of the men, Apsley Cherry-Garrard (left), later recounted the trip in a book called *The Worst Journey in the World*.

First to the Pole

Amundsen and his party set out for the pole on September 8, 1912, but soon returned because of the severe cold. They started again on October 19 and made good progress. Scott and his men left on November 1, but were hampered by their inability to ski well, their inexperience with sled dogs, the difficulties the ponies had walking on the snow, and the breakdown of their motor sleds. Amundsen's men skied 15–20 miles (24–32 km) a day, whereas Scott's men managed only 12 miles (19 km). Battling through icy blizzards, the Norwegians moved farther and farther ahead, and reached the South Pole on December 14.

TO SKI OR NOT TO SKI
Skis are faster than snowshoes and, because they spread weight, make it possible to cross thin ice. Coming from Norway, Amundsen and his men had skied all their lives. By contrast, Scott and his men were beginners at skiing, and their equipment, shown here, was old-fashioned.

Amundsen

Amundsen took approximately 50 dogs. Some would be killed to feed the other dogs.

Five Norwegians set out and all went to the pole.

Scott

Scott took 33 dogs, but all were sent back from the foot of the Beardmore Glacier.

Ten ponies went; all had to be killed before reaching the glacier.

Two motor sleds departed; both soon broke down.

Sixteen Britons set out; eight would go beyond the glacier, five to the pole.

LINING UP
From the start, Amundsen relied on only his men and his dogs. Scott, in contrast, sought to use motor sleds and ponies too, with poor results.

A Swift Ascent
A major challenge for both parties was ascending the Transantarctic Mountains via vast glaciers. On November 17, Amundsen's party reached the foot of the steep Axel Heiberg Glacier (left). Despite hauling 1 ton (900 kg) of supplies, they and their dogs reached the top in four days, having covered 44 miles (71 km) and climbed 10,000 feet (3,000 m).

Compass, thermometer, sundial, and (at bottom) barometer used by Scott

Battling up the Beardmore
Scott and his men chose to drag their sleds up the Beardmore Glacier to the summit 10,000 feet (3,000 m) above. Each man was pulling 200 pounds (91 kg); the snow was soft and the men frequently sank up to their knees in it. It took them more than three weeks to reach the top of the glacier.

The South Pole Conquered
On December 14, after carefully checking their compasses and the distance they had traveled, Amundsen and his men realized they had made it to the South Pole. Holding the post of a Norwegian flag, the men pushed it into the snowy ground and took photographs. The race was won! Although they did not know it, Scott was still 360 miles (580 km) behind them.

Meanwhile ...

While Scott's team was on its way back, six of his other men were marooned at Cape Adare, 300 miles (480 km) north of Ross Island. After a terrible winter in an ice cave, they made it back to base camp, but left much of their equipment (left) behind.

"Great God! This is an awful place."

ROBERT SCOTT, JOURNALS

Safe and Sound

On their return journey, Amundsen and his men enjoyed good weather and found the trip easy going. They arrived back at Framheim on January 25, 1912, with two sleds and 11 dogs, all fit and healthy. A few days later, they sailed for New Zealand.

NOBLE, BUT EXHAUSTING

Scott believed that "man-hauling" the sleds to the pole was nobler than using dogs. But dragging the heavy loads drained the strength of his men.

HEAVY GOING

On their way back, Scott and his men spent a day collecting rock samples on the Beardmore Glacier. These added over 31 pounds (14 kg) to the sleds, delaying the party further.

December 14, 1911:
Amundsen reaches pole

January 17, 1912:
Scott reaches pole

Polar Plateau

❶

OATES WALKS OUT

By mid-March, Oates was in constant pain from frostbite and ill from lack of food. Aware that he was hampering progress, on the morning of March 17 he walked out of the tent into a blizzard. He was never seen again.

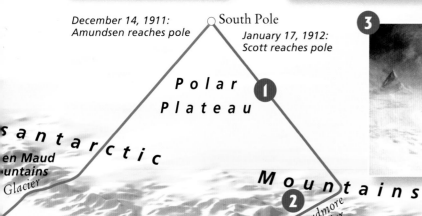

s a n t a r c t i c

en Maud
untains
Glacier

M o u n t a i n s

Mt Hope ▲   Beardmore Glacier

❷

February 17, 1912:
Evans dies

▲ Mt Markham

Shackleton Inlet

❸

A DESPERATE STRUGGLE

By the time Scott's party reached the South Pole, Amundsen and his men were already back on the Ross Ice Shelf. Turning for home, Scott realized he and his men faced "a desperate struggle."

R o s s   I c e   S h e l f

Cape Selborne

❹

LAST WORDS

Scott's last diary entry was dated March 29, 1912. Scott, Bowers, and Wilson died of cold and starvation, only 11 miles (18 km) from the next food store, One Ton Depot. A search party found their bodies on November 12.

March 17, 1912:
Oates dies

❹   □ Last camp
□ One Ton Depot

□ Cape Evans
Ross Island   ▲ Mt Erebus

S E A

DECEMBER | JANUARY 1912 | FEBRUARY | MARCH

8 Arrive at South Pole

14 Pass farthest point south reached by Shackleton

25 Return to Framheim

Amundsen cables his brother to say he has reached South Pole

7 News of Amundsen's triumph reported around the world **8**

12 Reach foot of Beardmore Glacier

6 Pass farthest point south reached by Shackleton

16 Realize the Norwegians have beaten them

17 Arrive at South Pole

19 Begin return trip

7 Reach head of Beardmore Glacier and begin descent

17 19 Reach foot of glacier

Evans dies

17 Oates dies

Approximate date deaths of Sc Wilson, and Bow

Triumph and Tragedy

Scott originally planned to take three men with him to the pole but changed his mind and took four: Henry Bowers, Edgar Evans, Lawrence Oates, and Edward Wilson. This proved to be a mistake: the tent was too small for five men, extra food was required, and cooking more food took longer. Hauling one sled bearing all their equipment, they struggled on. On January 16, they saw signs of Amundsen's party; a day later, they reached the pole and found the Norwegian flag. Demoralized, they turned homeward, but severe weather set in and all five men perished.

DISAPPOINTMENT AT THE POLE
The somber expressions on the faces of Scott and his men tell their story:
They had made it to the South Pole, but only after their rivals, the Norwegians.

The average temperature at the South Pole is −56°F (−49°C), and can be much lower as a result of wind chill. On the return trip, Scott's party experienced intense cold and blizzards.

FORGING AHEAD
Amundsen and his party set off almost two weeks before the British team. By the time Scott's expedition got underway, Amundsen was already more than 100 miles (160 km) ahead.

SOUTH POLE, ANTARCTICA
AVERAGE MONTHLY TEMPERATURE RANGE

°F		°C
86		30
68		20
50		10
32		0
14		-10
-4		-20
-22		-30
-40		-40
-58		-50
-76		-60
-94	J F M A M J J A S O N D	-70

Rockefeller Plateau

EDWARD VII LAND

Tran

Qu M

Axel Heibe

Creary Ice Rise

Roosevelt I.

☐ Framheim

Bay of Whales

R O S S

	SEPTEMBER 1911	OCTOBER		NOVEMBER	
AMUNDSEN & PARTY	**8** Set out for pole, but return because of severe cold	**19** Set out for pole again	**24** Arrive at 80°S	**17** Reach foot of mountains and start climb up Axel Heiberg Glacier, in warm weather	**21** Reach summit of glacier
SCOTT & PARTY		**1** Set out for pole		**18** Arrive at 80°S	

Antarctica Unveiled

Amundsen's achievement was celebrated around the world. Despite his failure, Scott was hailed as a hero in his day; later historians, however, criticized his poor decision-making. By the end of the Heroic Age of exploration, in 1917, less than 5 percent of Antarctica had been mapped. Since World War II, however, the use of aerial photography and satellite technology, as well as further pioneering treks by explorers including Ann Bancroft, Borge Ousland, and Phillip Law, have greatly expanded our knowledge of Antarctica. In the late 1950s, the international community took steps to protect the continent from territorial claims and exploitation, and preserve it for peaceful purposes. Today, it is visited not only by scientists, but also by increasing numbers of tourists.

AMUNDSEN'S FINAL JOURNEY
Amundsen, seen here at left congratulating American Richard Byrd on his 1926 flight over the North Pole, continued to explore the polar regions. But in 1928 his plane crashed in the Arctic and he disappeared without trace.

Antarctic Milestones

1928
Australian Sir Hubert Wilkins makes the first airplane flight over Antarctica.

1946-47
Operation Highjump, run by the US Navy, becomes the largest Antarctic Expedition ever mounted. More than 70,000 aerial photographs are taken.

1957-58
Major nations take part in the International Geophysical Year, collaborating on research projects. This leads to the Antarctic Treaty of 1959, which bans military activity and preserves the continent for scientific research.

1991
The Madrid Protocol forbids mining and mineral exploitation in Antarctica for the next 50 years and places strict environmental restrictions on tourism.

Later Heroes

The Heroic Age continued until the outbreak of World War I. One of the most remarkable later expeditions was the Australian Antarctic Expedition of 1911–14, led by Douglas Mawson, which mapped large areas of the coast. On one outing, one of Mawson's two companions fell into a crevasse, along with most of their dogs and supplies. Soon after, his remaining companion died and he had to march 100 miles (160 km) back to base alone.

In Their Footsteps

Antarctic tourism began in the 1950s and has increased rapidly in the last 25 years. A visit to Antarctica is the trip of a lifetime for many people, but the evergrowing numbers of visitors also represent a significant threat to Antarctica's fragile environment.

THE ANTARCTIC PIE

Anarctica has no government of its own, but seven countries claim slices of the continent: Argentina, Australia, Chile, France, New Zealand, Norway, and the United Kingdom. Most operate scientific bases within their claimed territory.

British Antarctic Territory
Argentina
Chile
Norway
Australian Antarctic Territory (Western Sector)
Terre Adélie (France)
Australian Antarctic Territory (Eastern Sector)
Ross Dependency (New Zealand)

Spirit of Adventure

In 1913, a large cross was erected on Observation Hill, near where Scott and his men died. It was inscribed with their names and the words "To strive, to seek, to find, and not to yield." This spirit of adventure lives on today in the work of the many scientists and explorers still investigating the wonders of this remote land.

ReFeRence

How Explorers Navigated

Navigation is the art of working out where you are and where you want to go by means of astronomy, mathematics, and/or specialized instruments. In the early days of exploration, sailors and other travelers used the position of the Sun, the planets, and the stars to guide them, especially when sailing out of sight of land where there were no other fixed reference points. Later, tools were invented that helped travelers navigate more accurately. A **compass** indicated which way was north. By comparing the direction of travel, according to the compass, to a compass drawn on a map, a traveler could plot his direction from place to place. A **telescope** allowed sailors and explorers to see landmarks from a great distance.

Compass used by Lewis and Clark

To plot position more accurately, however, explorers needed to determine their latitude and longitude. **Latitude** describes how far north or south you are, relative to the **equator**. **Longitude** describes your position east or west of the **Greenwich Meridian**, also known as the Prime Meridian or International Meridian, an imaginary line passing through the Royal Greenwich Observatory in London, England. Both are measured in degrees, and together they can pinpoint any location on Earth.

The equator (shown in red), Greenwich Meridian (orange), and lines of latitude and longitude (white).

To determine their latitude, explorers measured the height of the Sun at noon and then consulted printed tables that noted where the sun would be at noon at different latitudes and at different times of the year. Instruments for measuring the height of the Sun (relative to the instrument) included the **astrolabe** and the **quadrant**. These were, however, difficult to use accurately, especially in bad weather.

Early Persian astrolabe

To work out longitude required more precise measurements, and therefore more sophisticated instruments. The most widely used was the **sextant**, which appeared in the 18th century. This device incorporates two mirrors, a small telescope, and a sliding measuring scale. The user looks through the telescope at the horizon and moves the mirrors until the reflection of the Sun, Moon, or a particular star lines up with the horizon. The angle between the horizon and the Sun, Moon, or star can then be read off the measuring scale and, along with the precise time of day, checked against printed tables to obtain both the latitude and longitude.

Sextant belonging to David Livingstone

Although the **Global Positioning System (GPS)**, which uses satellites to pinpoint the user's location, has replaced sextants for day-to-day navigation, many modern sailors still take a sextant with them when they go to sea because it is not dependent on electricity or satellite technology, and therefore makes a reliable backup tool.

GPS navigation device

Cartography, the drawing of maps or charts, advanced alongside the development of navigational instruments. The maps drawn by explorers, such as those by Lewis and Clark, made an important contribution to later travelers' ability to find their way through the wilderness or across the oceans.

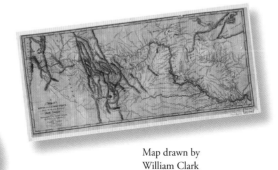

Map drawn by William Clark

Glossary

Arid
Very dry, or receiving little or no rain.

Artifact
An object made by a human being.

Cache
A hidden store of supplies. Explorers often buried or concealed caches of equipment for use on their return along the same route.

Crevasse
A deep, open crack in a glacier or ice field. If covered with snow, a crevasse can be difficult to detect.

Dehydration
Excessive loss of water from the body, usually as a result of heat and/or intense exercise.

Depot
A place for storing supplies.

Dormant
Temporarily inactive. A dormant plant is alive but not growing; a dormant animal is in a form of sleep.

Dysentery
A disease that causes severe diarrhea.

Inuits
The native people of northern Canada and parts of Greenland and Alaska.

Keelboat
A flat-bottomed riverboat.

Mangrove
A type of tree or shrub that grows in muddy swamps. Its tangled roots often stick out above the ground.

Missionary
A person who goes to another country to try to spread a religious faith.

Monsoon
The wet season in northern Australia, southern Asia, and central western Africa, which brings strong winds and heavy rainfall.

Palisade
A fence made of tall wooden stakes. This often formed the outer protective wall of a fort.

Pass
A gap or low area in a range of mountains where it is possible to cross the range.

Portage
To carry a boat and its cargo overland from one waterway to another.

Rift valley
A valley with steep sides, formed when land between two fractures in Earth's crust drops downward.

Scree
Small, loose stones on a mountainside or hillside.

Scurvy
An illness caused by a lack of vitamin C, which leads to bleeding under the skin, bleeding gums, and extreme weakness. Vitamin C is found in fresh fruit and vegetables, and also in seal meat.

Source
The place where a river starts flowing, usually a spring.

Stockade
An enclosure built using upright wooden posts or stakes.

Surveyor
Someone who examines and records the features of an area in order to make a map or plan.

Taproot
A straight plant root that grows downward, often with smaller rootlets attached to it.

Tectonic plate
A large segment of Earth's crust. Tectonic plates move constantly, though very slowly.

Terrain
An area of land, or the form of an area of land.

Transcontinental
Extending across a continent or continents.

Tributary
A river or stream that flows into a larger river or lake.

index

ABOUT THE AUTHOR

Dr. Betty Hagglund

Betty has spent many years studying and writing about exploration, and has published numerous books and articles on the topic. She grew up in the United States, not far from the spot where Lewis and Clark began their expedition, but now lives in England. She is a lecturer at the University of Birmingham, where she has taught courses on the history of travel and travel writing, and a Visiting Research Fellow at Nottingham Trent University, where she is involved with a research project on early 19th-century women explorers and scientists. A frequent traveler herself, she generally likes cold places better than hot ones, and would love to see Antarctica someday.

ACKNOWLEDGMENTS

Key t=top; l=left; r=right; tl=top left; tcl=top center left; tc=top center; tcr=top center right; tr=top right; cl=center left; c=center; cr=center right; b=bottom; bl=bottom left; bcl=bottom center left; bc=bottom center; bcr=bottom center right; br=bottom right

Photos
AGSA = Art Gallery of South Australia; AIRP = Air Photo North America; ALA = Alamy; APS = American Philosophical Society; AR = Smithsonian American Art Museum/Art Resource; AUS = Auscape; BA = Bridgeman Art Library; BLYA = Yale Collection of Western Americana; CBT = Corbis; DP = burkeandwills.net.au; GI = Getty Images; HH = Hedgehog House; IS = iStock Photo; LC = Library of Congress; NSF = NASA Space Flight; NLA = National Library of Australia; NMA = National Museum of Australia; RGS = Royal Geographical Society; SH = Shutterstock; SI = Smithsonian Institute; SLNSW = State Library of NSW; SLV = State Library of Victoria; TF = Top Foto; TPL = The Photo Library; TRANZ = Tranz International Image Library

7bl ALA; tr BA; cl BLYALE; br, tr CBT; cr GI; 8bl AR; tr CBT; 9tr APS; bc CBT; tc GI; br, cr TPL; 10br AR; tc CBT; 11cr CBT; br iS; tr SH; bl TPL; tl TRANZ; 12br AIRP; tl CBT; 13cc, cl, tr CBT; br LC; 14b iS; cr, tr TPL; 15br, tl APS; cc CBT; tr GI; br SH; 16tc AIRP; br TPL; 17br, cc CBT; tc, LC; cl SH; br, cc, cc TPL; 18br GI; cc TF; 19tr CBT; bl GI; cr RGS; br TPL; 20tc GI; br RGS; 21bl GI; tr RGS; br TF; c, cr TPL; 23tl GI; bc RGS; cr TPL; 24bl CBT; cc, cr, tl TPL; 25tc TF; bl TPL; 26cr CBT; bc, bl GI; 27tr, CBT; cr, cr, RGS; tc SI; bc TRANZ; 28 tc GI; br TPL; 29bl GI; bc, tl, tr RGS; bc TF; br TPL; 30bc GI; tr TF; cr TPL; 31tr CBT; br GI; tl SI; bc, cc, cc TPL; 32tc AGSA; br SLV; 33cl NLA; tl SLNSW; bc, br, br SLV; 34tr NLA; cr SLNSW; bc SLV; 35cr NLA; br, c SLV; bc, tc TPL; 36bl AUS; tr SH; 37tr GI; cl SLV; 38br NMA; tc TPL; 39c ALA; br SH; tc SLV; bl TPL; 40bc, tr AUS; cr TPL; 41bc, c NLA; 42bl SH; cl SLNSW; br SLV; 43cr NLA; br SLV; 44cl SLV; bl TPL; 45bc, cc, tc SLV; cr TF; 46bc, bc, tc SLV; 47 br DP; bc, tl NLA; cc, tr SLV; 48b NLA; br RGS; tc TPL; 49bc, cl RGS; tl TF; 50br RGS; bl, tl TF; 51cl, tl RGS; cr TF; br TPL; 52t HH; br RGS; 53tc CBT; bc, cc, cr GI; tl HH; cc TF; cc TPL; 54cr TF; bl TPL; 55br GI; cl HH; bl TF; cl TPL; 56bc, tc TF; 57c GI; tl HH; cl RGS; br, cr, tr TF; 58cr CBT; tc HH; cr TPL; 59tc, tr ALA; br, br NSF; cc, cl TF.

Illustrations
Peter Bull Art Studio 6t, 18t, 22bl, 37tr, 41tr, 42-3b, 45b, 52cr, 55t, 56-7b; Andrew Davies/Creative Communication 8cr, 9bl, 13b, 19t, 38cr.

Cartography by Will Pringle.

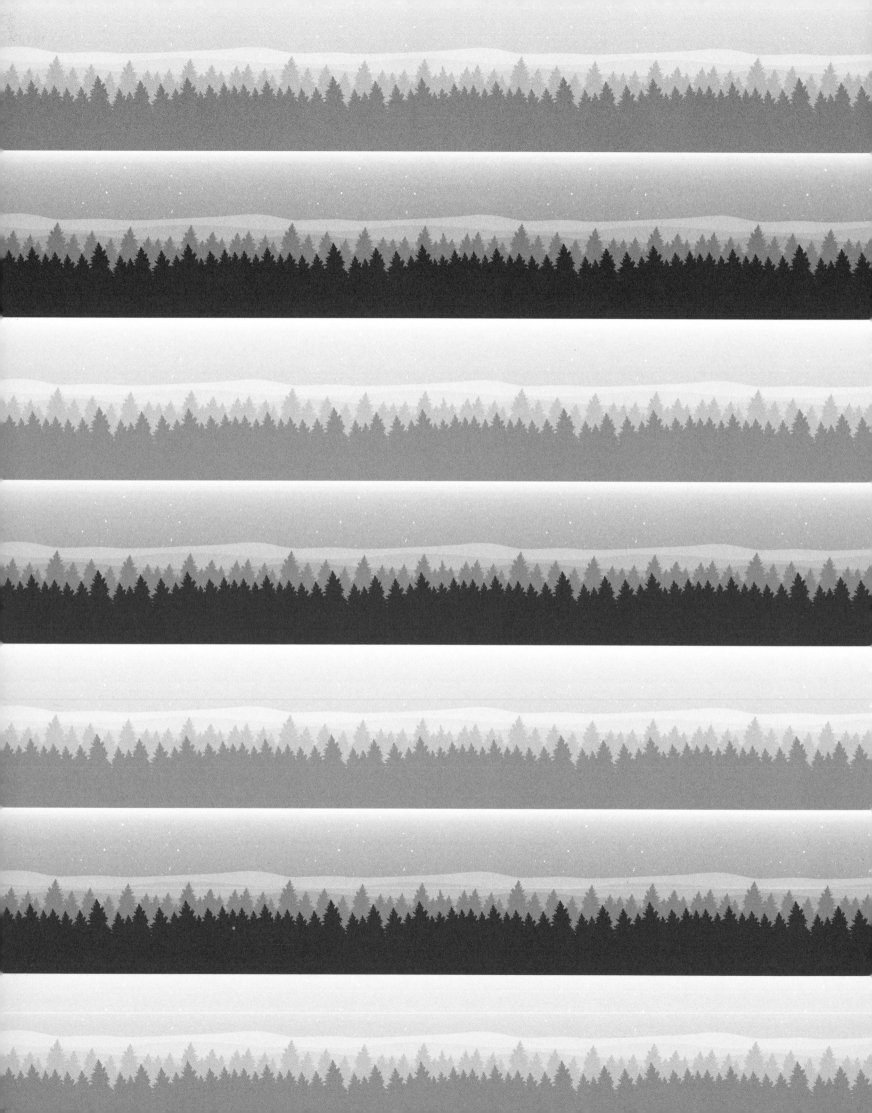